# Easy Concert Pieces
## Leichte Konzertstücke

for Piano
für Klavier

Volume 1 / Band 1:
50 Easy Pieces from 5 Centuries
50 leichte Stücke aus 5 Jahrhunderten

Edited by / Herausgegeben von
Rainer Mohrs and / und Monika Twelsiek

CD-Einspielung: Vera Sacharowa

**ED 22547**
ISMN 979-0-001-16904-0
ISBN 978-3-7957-1013-2

Volume 2 / Band 2:
ED 22548

Mainz · London · Berlin · Madrid · New York · Paris · Prague · Tokyo · Toronto
© 2016 SCHOTT MUSIC GmbH & Co. KG, Mainz · Printed in Germany

# Preface

The 'Easy Concert Pieces' series presents easy piano pieces in progressive order. These pieces are intended to complement a piano tutorial method and are particularly suitable for performance at auditions, concerts, competitions and examinations. They offer varied repertoire in a broad selection of pieces from the Baroque, Classical, Romantic and Modern eras.

Volume 1 contains pieces in the five-note range and easy pieces spanning a single octave. Other criteria for selection are simple rhythms and very easy chords. Crossing the thumb underneath, playing several parts together and pedalling are not yet required.

Volume 2 contains pieces with an extended range of two octaves. Crossing the thumb under, pedal use, simple polyphony and three- or four-part chords all feature here, as do simple ornaments, playing cantabile and differentiating between melody and accompaniment.

Volume 3 is intended for advanced players who wish to work on expressive playing and individual interpretation. These pieces demand greater fluency and rhythmic control, more advanced articulation and phrasing, polyphonic harmonies (playing several parts even with one hand) and differentiation of tone and touch.

# Vorwort

Die Reihe „Easy Concert Pieces" enthält leichte Klavierstücke in progressiver Reihenfolge. Die Stücke sind als Ergänzung zur Klavierschule gedacht und eignen sich besonders für das Vorspiel an Musikschulen, für Wettbewerbe und für Prüfungen. Die Repertoireauswahl ist vielseitig und bietet eine vielfältige Auswahl an Stücken aus Barock, Klassik, Romantik und Moderne.

Band 1 enthält Stücke im Fünftonraum und leichte Stücke im einfachen Oktavraum. Weitere Kriterien für die Auswahl waren einfache Rhythmik und sehr leichtes Akkordspiel. Daumenuntersatz, polyphone Mehrstimmigkeit und Pedalspiel werden noch nicht vorausgesetzt.

Band 2 enthält Stücke im erweiterten Tonumfang von 2 Oktaven. Vorausgesetzt werden Daumenuntersatz, Pedalspiel, einfache Polyphonie und drei- bis vierstimmiges Akkordspiel, einfache Verzierungen, cantables Spiel und Differenzierung zwischen Melodie und Begleitung.

Band 3 wendet sich an fortgeschrittene Spieler, die an ausdrucksvollem Spiel und eigenständiger Interpretation arbeiten wollen. Die Stücke stellen höhere Ansprüche an Geläufigkeit und Rhythmik, Artikulation und Phrasierung, polyphones Spiel (Mehrstimmigkeit auch in einer Hand) und die klangliche Differenzierung des Klaviersatzes.

Rainer Mohrs / Monika Twelsiek
English translation Julia Rushworth

# Contents / Inhalt

# Part I: Pieces in five-note range

Teil I: Stücke im Fünftonraum

## Old German Dance

### Alter deutscher Tanz

Michael Praetorius
1571–1621

# Canario

Joachim von der Hofe
1567?–1620

**2**

# Minuetto

Alexander Reinagle
1756–1809

3

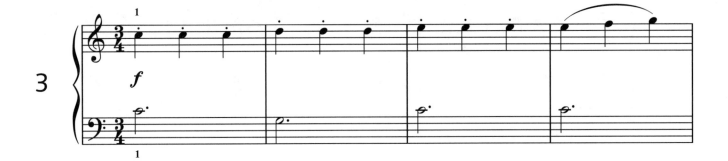

from / aus: A. Reinagle, 24 Short and Easy Pieces, No. 1

# Allegro

Alexander Reinagle

4

*Fine*

*D.C. al Fine*

from / aus: A. Reinagle, 24 Short and Easy Pieces, No. 4

# Little Sonata
## Kleine Sonate

1st movement / 1. Satz

Charles Henry Wilton
1761–1832

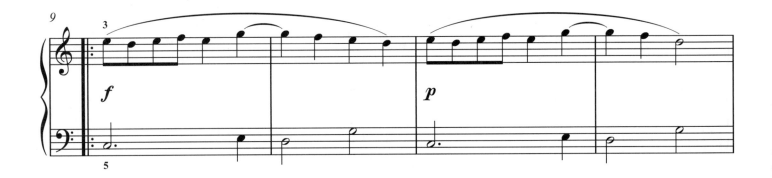

# A Midsommer Day's Song

## Sommertagslied

Cornelius Gurlitt
1820–1903

from / aus: C. Gurlitt, The friend of the family / Der Hausfreund op. 197

# Dreary Hours

## Trübe Stunden

Cornelius Gurlitt

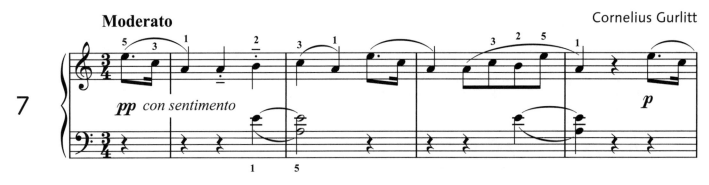

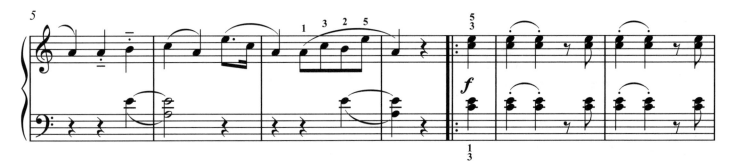

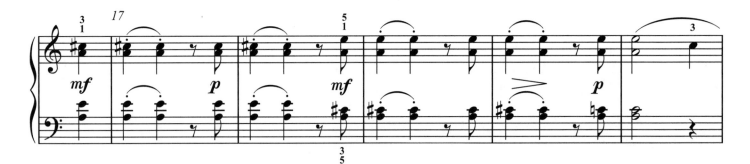

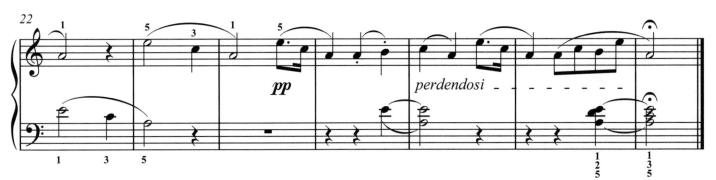

from / aus: C. Gurlitt, The friend of the family / Der Hausfreund op. 197

13

# The Hurdy-Gurdy Man

## Der Leierkastenmann

Georges Frank Humbert
1892–1958

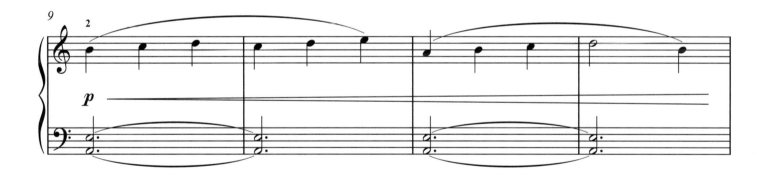

from / aus: G. F. Humbert, Magic Hours / Zauberstunden, Schott ED 2379

# The Train

## Die Eisenbahn

Georges Frank Humbert

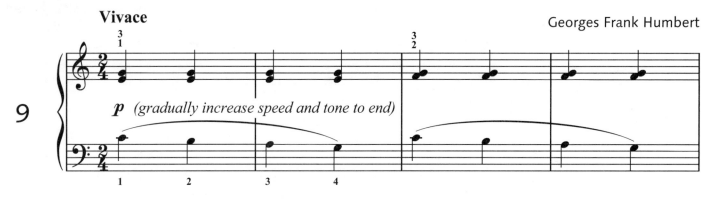

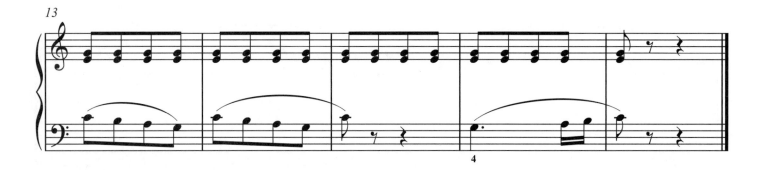

from / aus: G. F. Humbert, Toys / Allerlei Spielzeug, Schott ED 2605

# The Snake Charmer

## Der Schlangenbeschwörer

Georges Frank Humbert

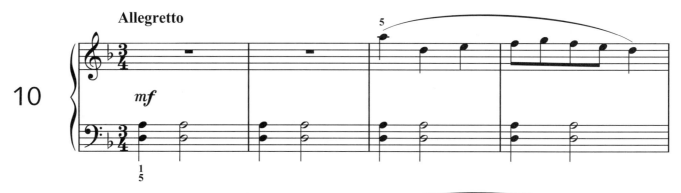

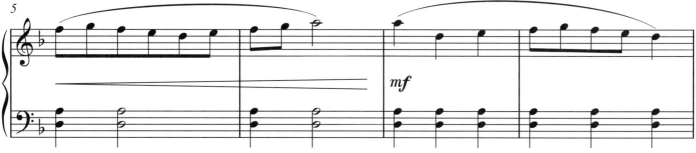

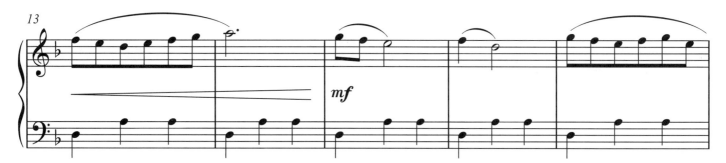

from / aus: G. F. Humbert, Magic Hours / Zauberstunden, Schott ED 2379

11 CD

# Tarantella

Georges Frank Humbert

**Con moto**

11

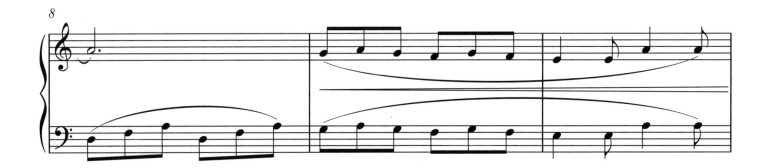

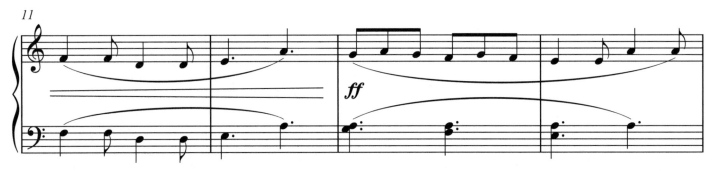

from / aus: G. F. Humbert, Magic Hours / Zauberstunden, Schott ED 2379

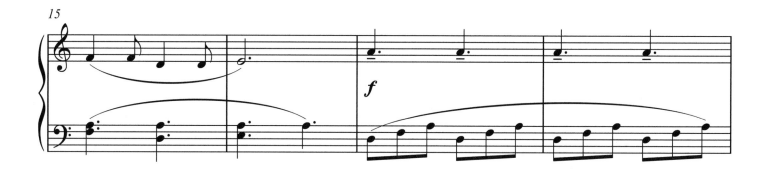

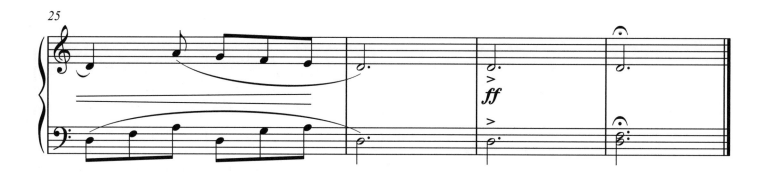

# On the Way

## Auf dem Marsche

Georges Frank Humbert

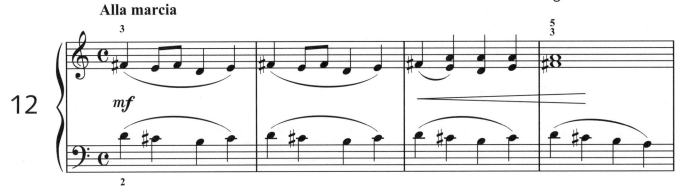

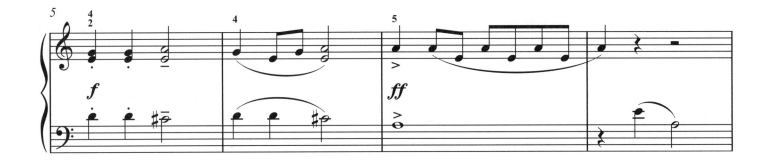

from / aus: G. F. Humbert, Magic Hours / Zauberstunden, Schott ED 2379

# Ragtime

Georges Frank Humbert

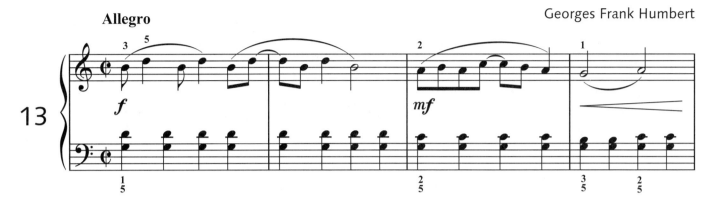

**13**

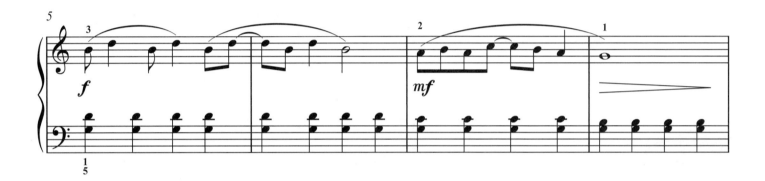

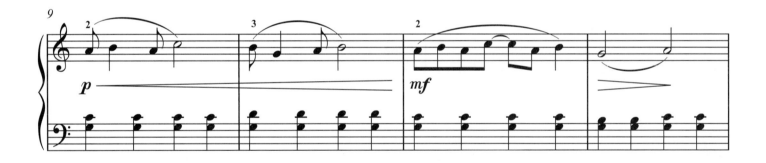

Original title: The Dancing Negro / Originaltitel: Der tanzende Neger

# Dialogue

## Dialog

Fritz Emonts
1920–2003

**14**

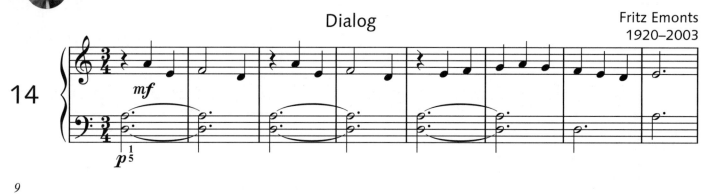

# Changing Time

## Taktwechsel

Fritz Emonts

**15**

To avoid page turn problems, this page stays empty.
Aus wendetechnischen Gründen bleibt diese Seite leer.

# For the Young

## Für die Jugend

Piano Piece No. 1 / Klavierstück Nr. 1

Marko Tajčevič
1900–1984

**16**

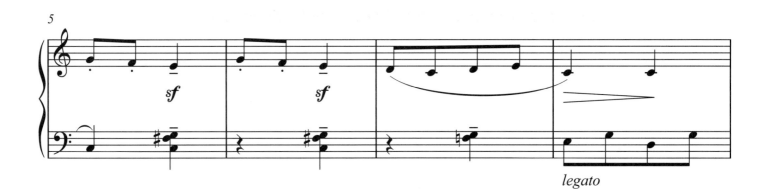

from / aus: M. Tajčevič, Piano Works / Klavierwerke, Vol. 1, Schott ED 21074

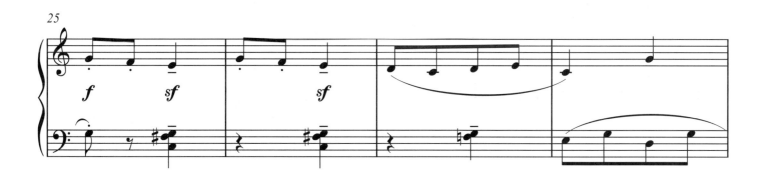

# Basso ostinato

Henk Badings
1907–1987

**17**

Andante ♩ = 120

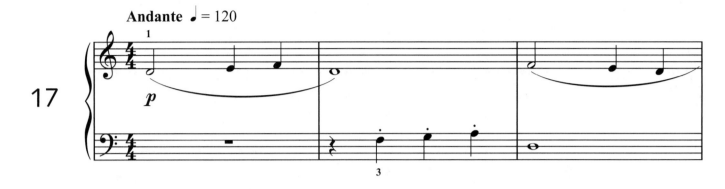

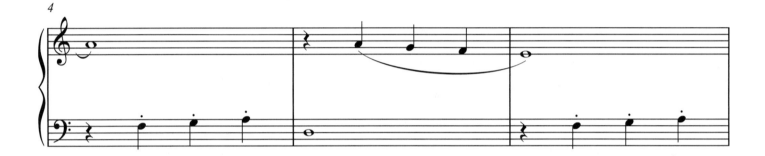

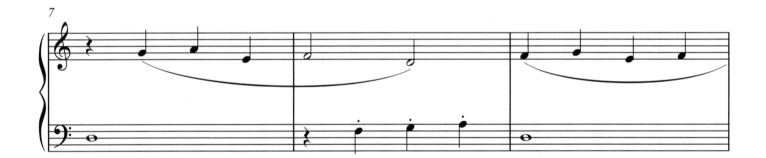

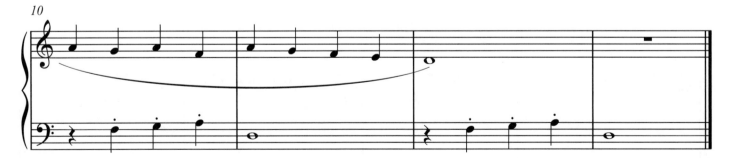

from / aus: H. Badings, Arcadia, Vol. 1, 10 Five-note pieces on white keys / 10 Fünfton-Stücke auf weißen Tasten, Schott ED 4176

# Here Comes the Caravan

## Die Karawane zieht vorbei

Rainer Mohrs
*1953

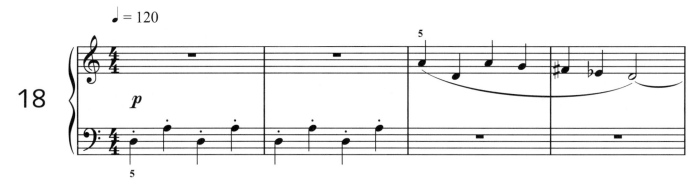

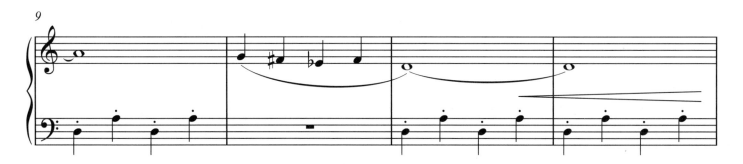

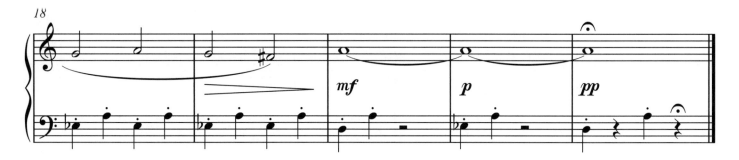

# Folk Dance in the Mountains

## Volkstanz in den Bergen

Rainer Mohrs

**19**

*) Repetition: e flat / Wiederholung: es

# Shepherd's Melody

Rainer Mohrs

## Hirtenmelodie

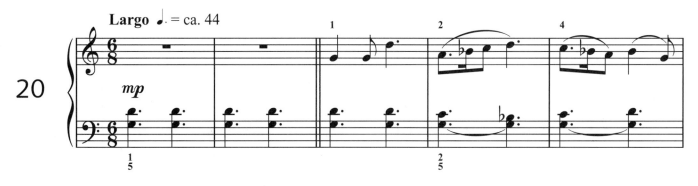

Fine

*D.C. al Fine*

# Rock Piano Fever

Hans-Günter Heumann
* 1955

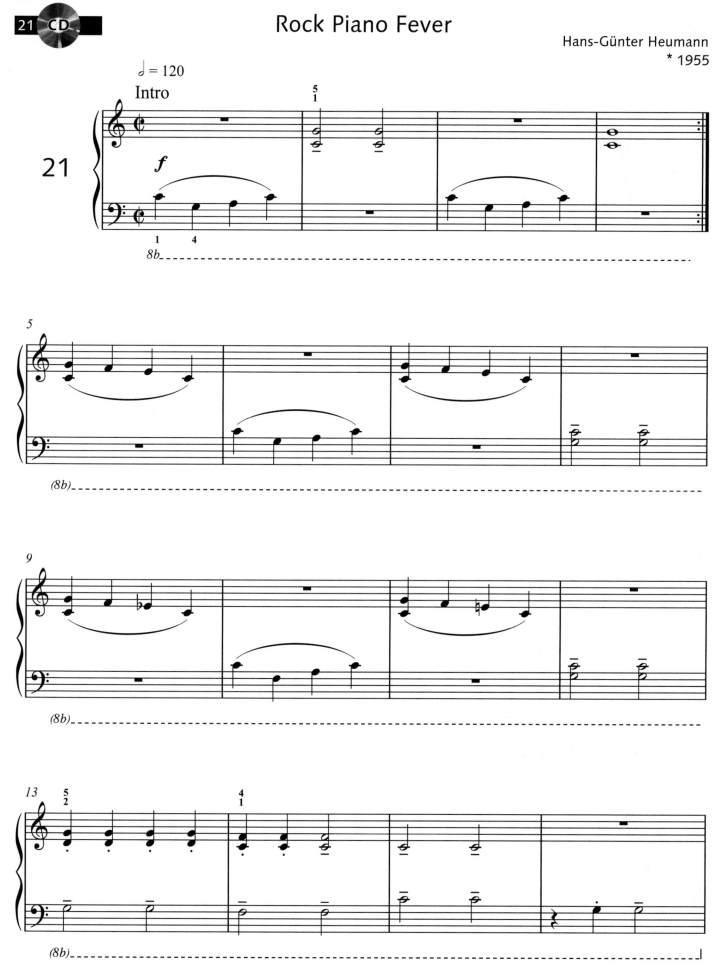

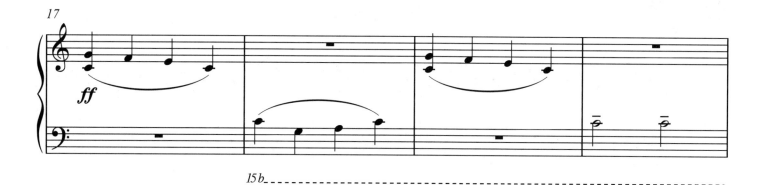

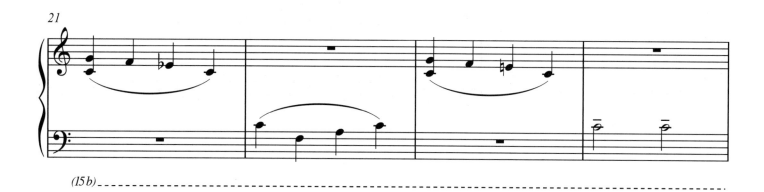

15b

(15b)

(15b)

(15b)

# Part II: Different five-note ranges and octave range
## Teil II: Wechselnder Fünftonraum und leichter Oktavraum

22 CD

## Allemande

Johann Hermann Schein
1586–1630

23 CD

## Aria

Daniel Speer
1636–1707

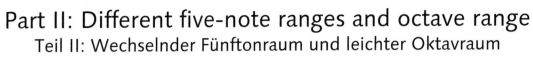

# Menuett
## A minor / a-Moll

Johann Krieger
1651–1735

**24**

*)

# Bourrée
## E minor / e-Moll

Christoph Graupner
1683–1760

**25**

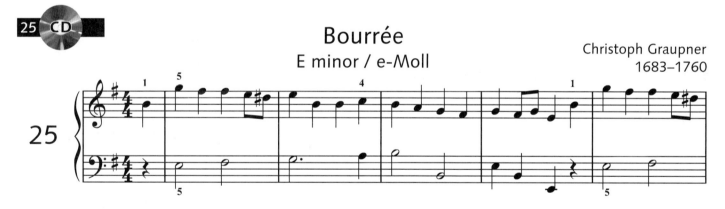

# Menuett
## D major / D-Dur

Jean-Philippe Rameau
1683–1764

**26**

# Musette

### D major / D-Dur

Johann Sebastian Bach
1685–1750

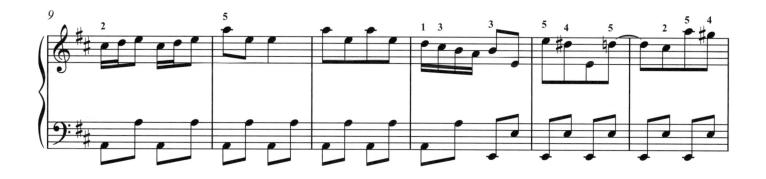

*Fine*

*D. C. al Fine*

from / aus:  / Notebook for Anna Magdalena Bach / Notenbüchlein für Anna Magdalena Bach, Schott ED 2698

# Gavotte

## C major / C-Dur

Georg Friedrich Händel
1685–1759

**28**

*(4)*

*(8)*

*(12)*

*)

# Four Little Pieces

## Vier kleine Stücke

### I Entrée

Daniel Gottlob Türk
1756–1813

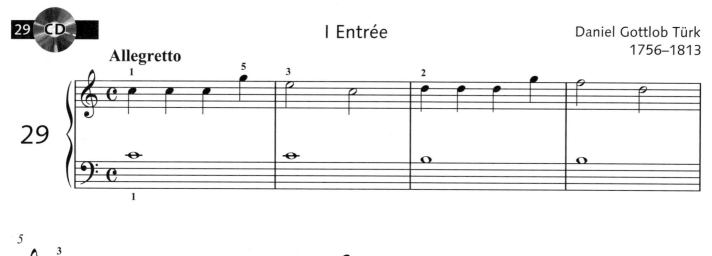

### II Minuetto

Daniel Gottlob Türk

## III I am so Dull and Ill

## Ich bin so matt und krank

Daniel Gottlob Türk

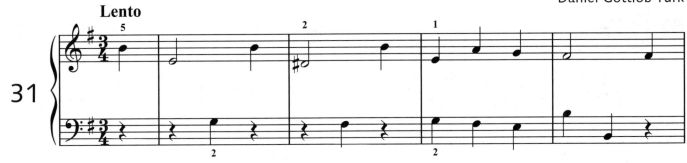

## IV A Carefree Fellow

## Hanns ohne Sorgen

Daniel Gottlob Türk

# Three Little Pieces

## Drei kleine Stücke

Antonio Diabelli
1781–1858

I

**33**

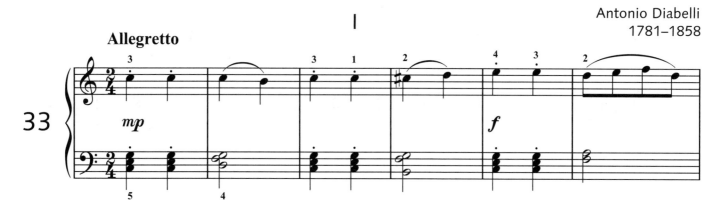

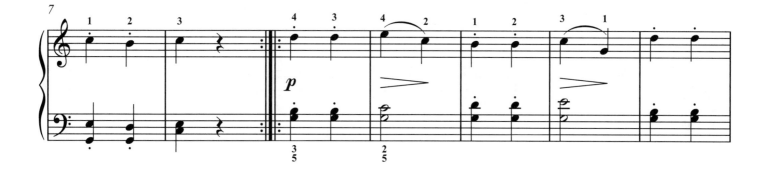

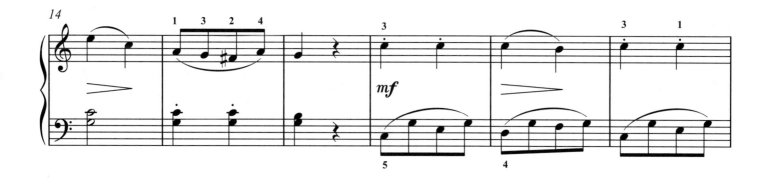

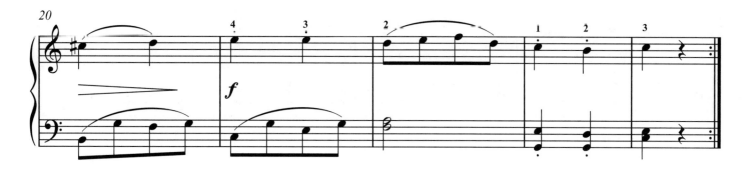

# II

Antonio Diabelli

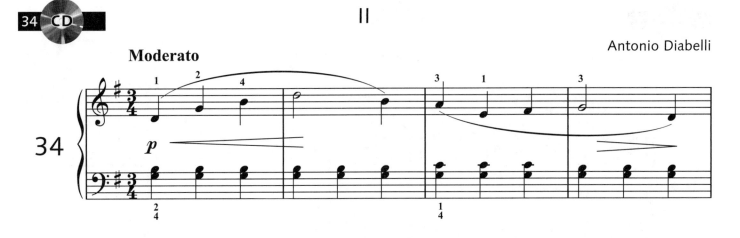

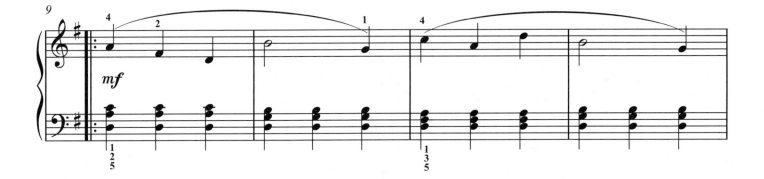

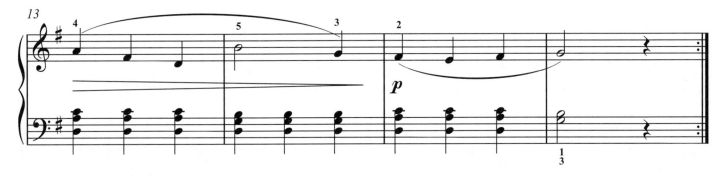

# III

Antonio Diabelli

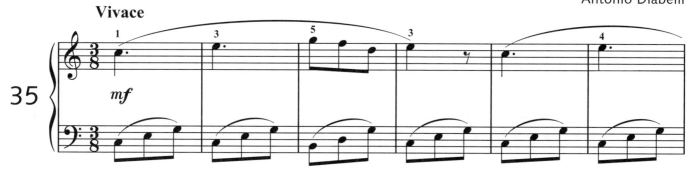

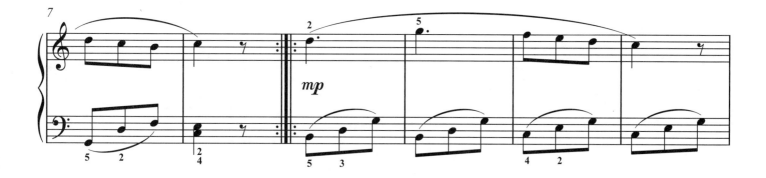

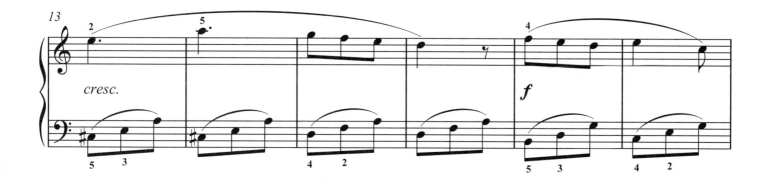

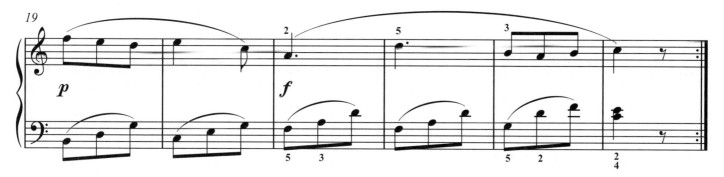

# A Little Piece
## Stückchen

Robert Schumann
1810–1856

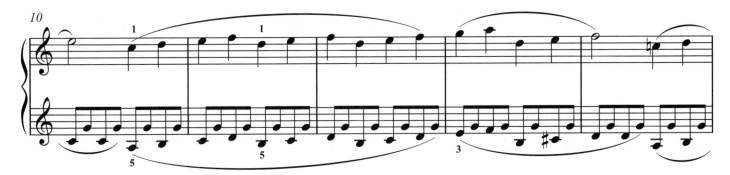

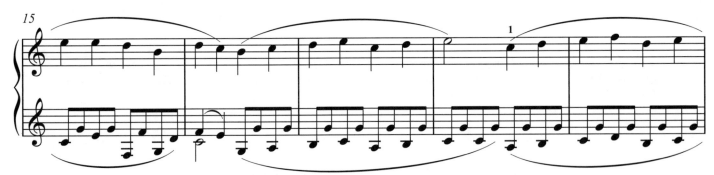

from / aus: R. Schumann, Album for the Young / Album für die Jugend, op. 68, Schott ED 9010

# Song without Words

## Lied ohne Worte

Fritz Spindler
1816–1905

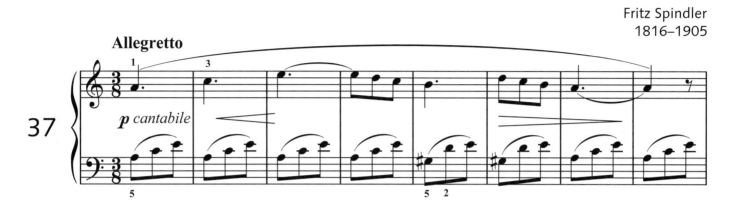

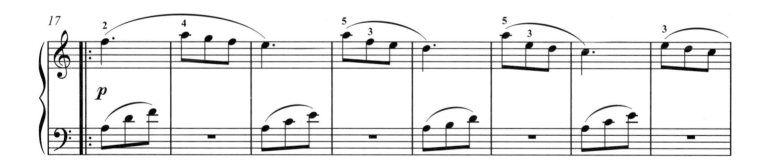

# Dolly's Complaint

## Der Puppe Klagelied

César Franck
1822–1890

from / aus: C. Franck: 18 Short Pieces / 18 kurze Stücke

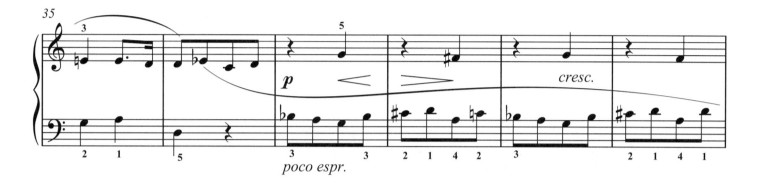

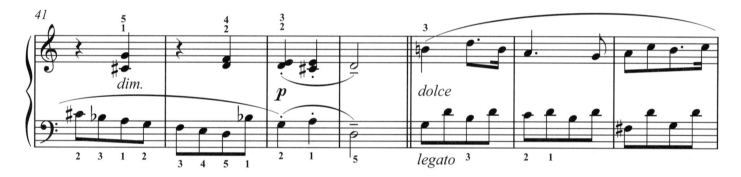

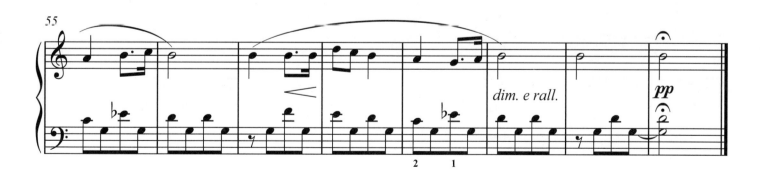

# Fairy Tale

## Ein kleines Märchen

Alexander Gretchaninoff
1864–1956

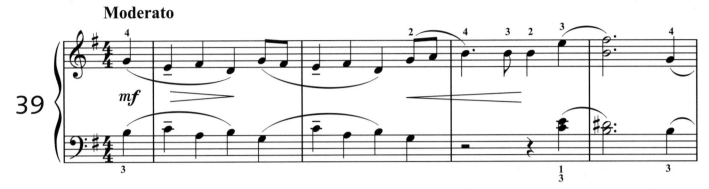

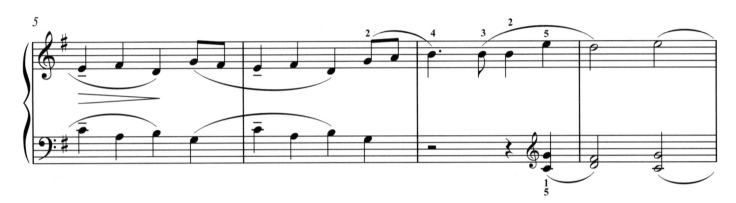

from / aus: A. Gretchaninoff, Children's Book / Das Kinderbuch op. 98, Schott ED 1100

# Njanja is ill

## Njanja ist krank

Alexander Gretchaninoff

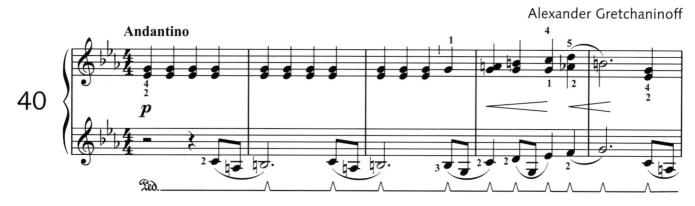

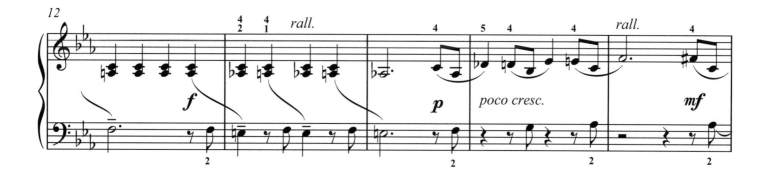

from / aus: A. Gretchaninoff, Children's Book / Das Kinderbuch op. 98, Schott ED 1100

# A Tiresome Lesson

### Eine langweilige Schularbeit

Alexander Gretchaninoff

bored / gelangweilt

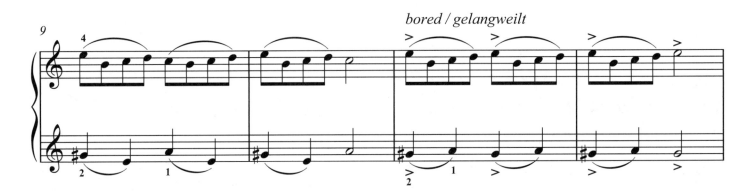

from / aus: A. Gretchaninoff, Children's Book / Das Kinderbuch op. 98, Schott ED 1100

# Dancing Piece

### Tanzstück

Carl Orff
1895–1982

42

*p*

1. 2.

*Fine*

*f*

*D. C. al Fine*

from / aus: C. Orff, Klavier-Übung, Schott ED 3561

# Piano Study

### Klavier-Übung

Carl Orff

43

*Fine*

*D. C. al Fine*

from / aus: C. Orff, Klavier-Übung, Schott ED 3561 (No. 15)

# Tango

Fritz Emonts
1920–2003

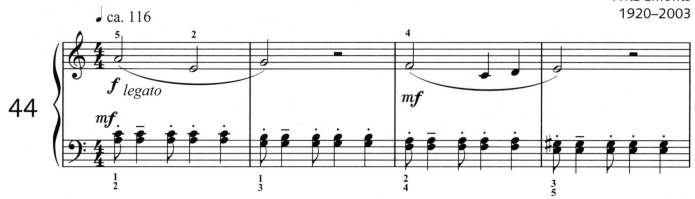

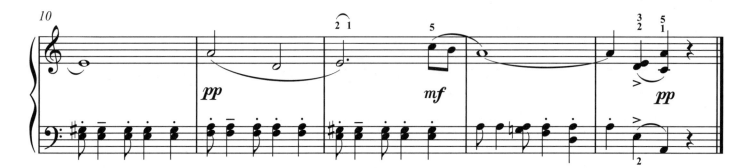

# Bagpipes

## Dudelsack

♩ = ca. 132

Fritz Emonts

**45**

from / aus: F. Emonts, Playing with five notes / Spiel mit fünf Tönen, Schott ED 5285

# Elephants
## Elefanten

Gunter Kretschmer
1935–2012

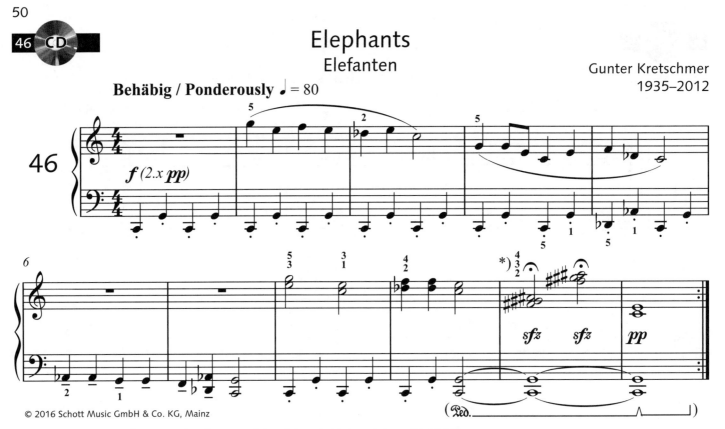

from / aus: G. Kretschmer, In the Playground / Auf dem Spielplatz, Schott ED 20648

\*) You can have the elephants do a trick here.
\*) Hier kannst du die Elefanten ein Kunststück machen lassen.

# Rainy Weather Blues

## Regenwetter-Blues

Gunter Kretschmer

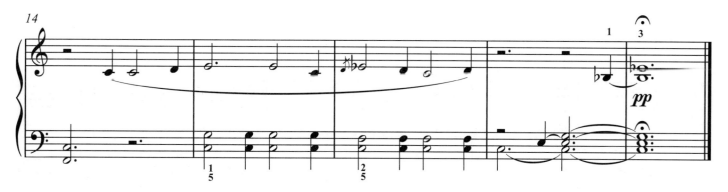

from / aus: G. Kretschmer, In the Playground / Auf dem Spielplatz, Schott ED 20648

# Tales from the Arabian Nights

## Märchen aus 1001 Nacht

Barbara Heller
*1936

**48**

from / aus: B. Heller, Sound Traces / Klangspuren, Vol. 1, Schott ED 21577

# Holidays

Marianne Magolt
*1953

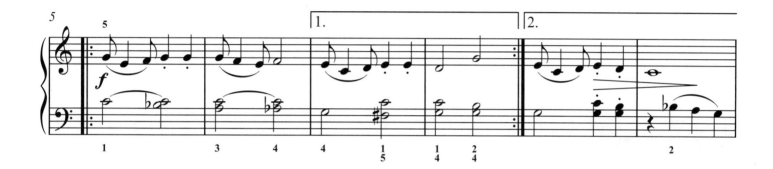

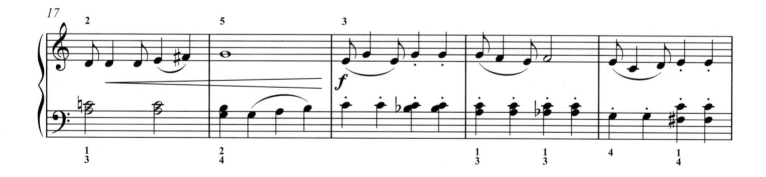

# The Spanish Guitar Player

## Der spanische Gitarrenspieler

Mike Schoenmehl
* 1957

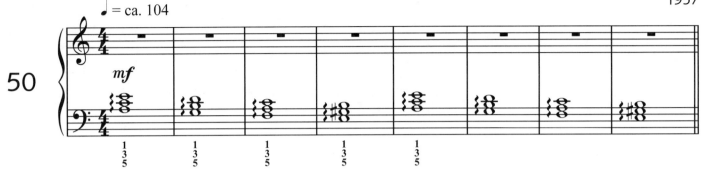

Schott Music, Mainz 57575

from / aus: M. Schoenmehl, Little Stories in Jazz, Schott ED 7186

When you play the last note, you shout 'olé' as you may
have heard it when listening to Spanish Folklore.

Mit dem letzten Ton rufst du „olé" wie du es vielleicht schon
einmal bei spanischer Volksmusik gehört hast.